Pebble® Plus

All About Sharks

# Hammerhead Sharks

by Deborah Nuzzolo

CAPSTONE PRESS
a capstone imprint

W9-DDZ-393

Pebble Plus is published by Capstone Press,
1710 Roe Crest Drive, North Mankato, Minnesota 56003
www.mycapstone.com

**Library of Congress Cataloging-in-Publication Data**
Names: Nuzzolo, Deborah, author.
Title: Hammerhead sharks / by Deborah Nuzzolo.
Description: North Mankato, Minnesota : Capstone Press, [2017] | Series:
Pebble plus. All about sharks | Audience: Ages 4–8. | Audience: K to grade 3. |
Includes bibliographical references and index.
Identifiers: LCCN 2016059066| ISBN 9781515770039 (library binding) |
ISBN 9781515770091 (pbk.) | ISBN 9781515770152 (ebook (pdf)).
Subjects: LCSH: Hammerhead sharks—Juvenile literature. | CYAC: Sharks.
Classification: LCC QL638.95.S7 B35 2018 | DDC 597.3/4—dc23
LC record available at https://lccn.loc.gov/2016059066

**Editorial Credits**
Nikki Bruno Clapper, editor; Kayla Rossow, designer;
Kelly Garvin, media researcher; Gene Bentdahl, production specialist

**Photo Credits**
Seapics: Andre Seale, 19, Martin Strmiska, 15; Shutterstock: City of Angeis, 13, divedog,
24, frantisekhojdusz, 1, 21, Joost van Uffelen, 5, Martin Prochazkacz, 9, Matt9122, 11,
nicolasvoisin44, cover, Rich Carey, 2, Tomas Kotouc, 7, Willyam Bradberry, 23; Superstock/
Norbert Probst/imageb/imageBROKER, 17

**Artistic elements**
Shutterstock: Apostrophe, HorenkO, Magenta10

## Note to Parents and Teachers

The All About Sharks set supports national curriculum standards for
science related to the characteristics and behavior of animals. This book
describes and illustrates hammerhead sharks. The images support early
readers in understanding the text. The repetition of words and phrases
helps early readers learn new words. This book also introduces early
readers to subject-specific vocabulary words, which are defined in the
Glossary section. Early readers may need assistance to read some words
and to use the Table of Contents, Glossary, Read More, Internet Sites,
Critical Thinking Questions, and Index sections of the book.

Printed in the United States of America.
0531

# Table of Contents

# Searching the Sand

A shark watches the seafloor.

It finds a stingray in the sand.

The shark uses its wide head
to trap the stingray. Chomp!

The shark takes a bite.

4

Hammerhead sharks live in warm, shallow seas. They swim alone or in groups called schools.

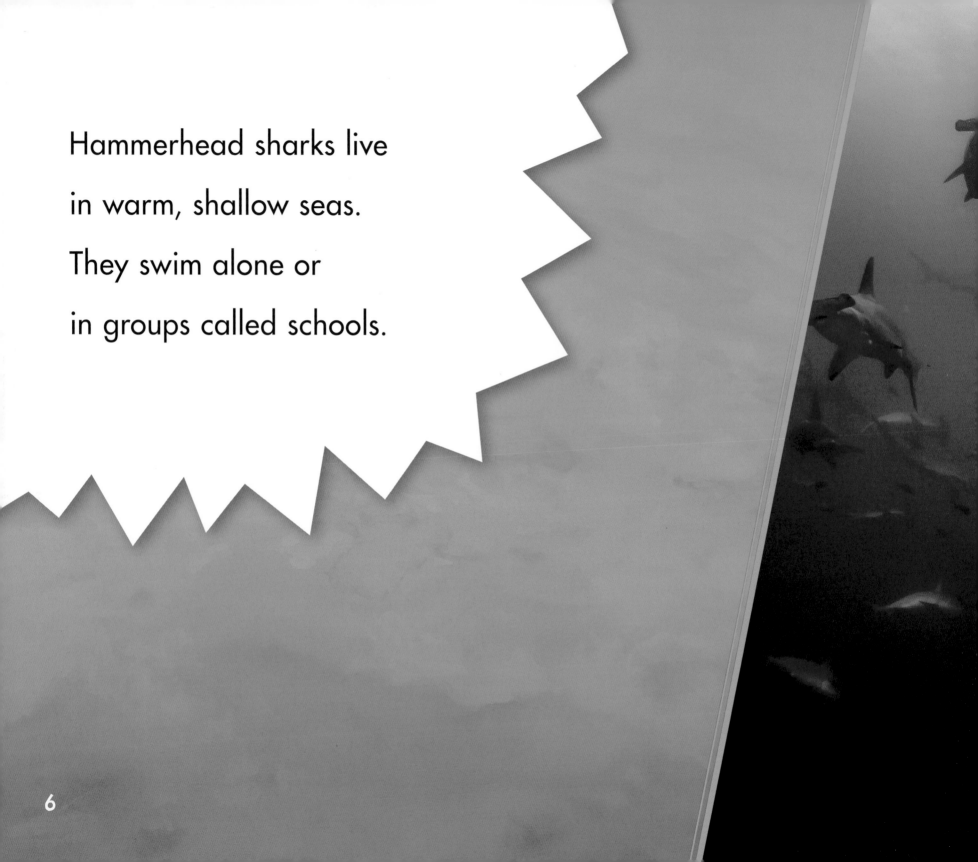

# A Hammer for a Head

A hammerhead has an eye

at each end of its head.

This shark can see

a large area more quickly

than most other sharks can.

A hammerhead shark has two dorsal fins on its back. Dorsal fins help sharks stay balanced when they swim.

dorsal fins

Nine kinds of hammerheads swim in the sea. Bonnetheads are the smallest. Great hammerheads are the largest.

bonnethead
5 feet (1.5 meters)

great hammerhead
15 feet (4.6 meters)

5 feet (1.5 meters)

bonnethead

# Hunting and Eating

Hammerhead sharks hunt smaller fish and stingrays. They also eat crabs, squid, and lobsters.

The hammerhead shark's head has special organs. These organs help the shark find nearby prey.

# Hammerhead Babies

Hammerhead shark pups are born live. Between 6 and 50 pups are born at one time. The pups have rounded heads.

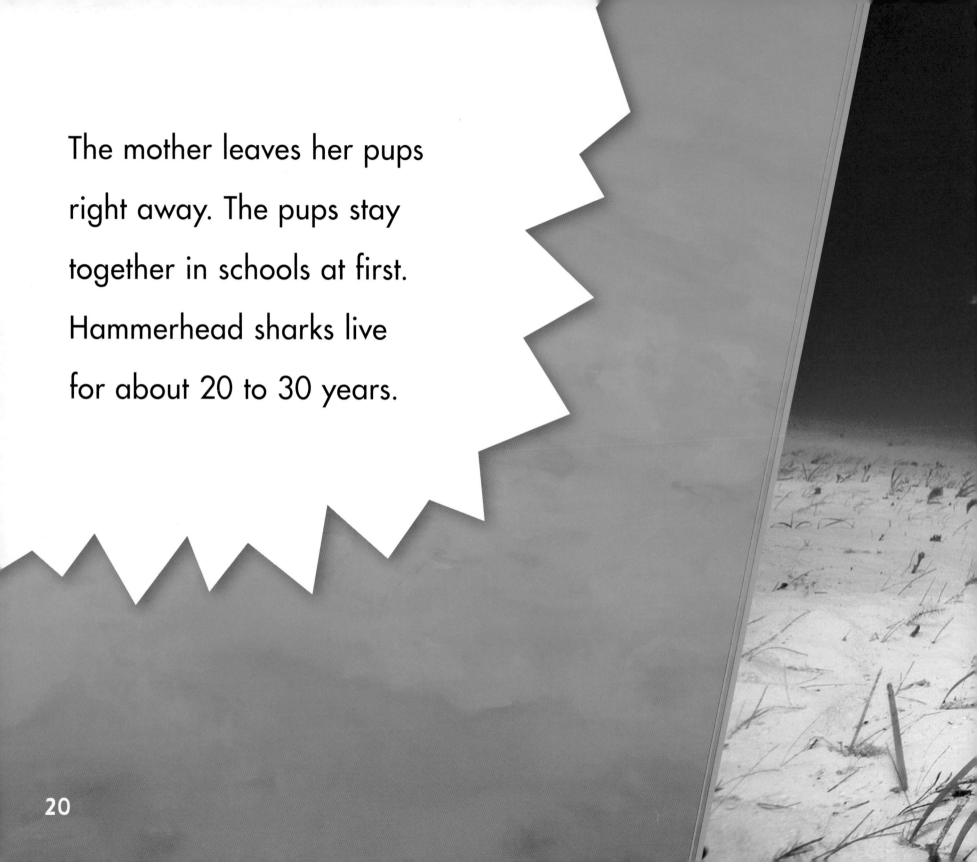

The mother leaves her pups right away. The pups stay together in schools at first. Hammerhead sharks live for about 20 to 30 years.

# Glossary

**balanced**—steady and not falling over

**dorsal fin**—a fin located on the back

**escape**—to get away from

**hunt**—to find and catch animals for food

**organ**—a body part that does a certain job

**prey**—an animal hunted by another animal for food

**prowl**—to move around quietly and secretly

**pup**—a young shark

**school**—a large number of the same kind of fish swimming and feeding together

**shallow**—not deep

**stingray**—a fish that has a flat body, fins that look like wings, and a long, poisonous tail

# Read More

**Barnes, Nico.** *Hammerhead Sharks.* Sharks. Minneapolis: Abdo Kids, 2015.

**Meister, Cari.** *Sharks.* Life Under the Sea. Minneapolis: Jump!, 2014.

**Morey, Allan.** *Hammerhead Sharks.* Sharks. Mankato, Minn.: Amicus Ink, 2017.

# Internet Sites

FactHound offers a safe, fun way to find Internet sites related to this book. All of the sites on FactHound have been researched by our staff.

Here's all you do:

Visit *www.facthound.com*

Type in this code: 9781515770039

**Super-cool stuff!** Check out projects, games and lots more at **www.capstonekids.com**

# Critical Thinking Questions

1. How do hammerhead sharks catch stingrays?

2. How are hammerhead sharks different from other sharks?

3. What do hammerhead sharks eat?

# Index